50 French Diner Recipes

By: Kelly Johnson

Table of Contents

- Croque Monsieur
- Quiche Lorraine
- French Onion Soup
- Ratatouille
- Steak Frites
- Coq au Vin
- Duck Confit
- Beef Bourguignon
- Escargots de Bourgogne
- Moules Marinières
- Croissant Sandwiches
- Gratin Dauphinois
- Salade Niçoise
- Poulet Rôti (Roast Chicken)
- Tarte Tatin
- Chateaubriand
- French Toast

- Bœuf en Croûte (Beef Wellington)
- French-style Omelette
- Soupe au Pistou
- Pâté en Croûte
- Galette Bretonne
- Croque Madame
- Cassoulet
- Pissaladière
- Foie Gras
- Salmon en Papillote
- Clafoutis
- Endives au Gratin
- Blanquette de Veau
- Pâtisserie au Chocolat
- Pommes Frites
- Soufflé au Fromage
- Chouquettes
- Grilled Ratatouille Sandwich
- Pain Perdu (French Toast)

- Salade de Chèvre Chaud
- Mousse au Chocolat
- Bouillabaisse
- French Garlic Butter Shrimp
- Potatoes Lyonnaise
- Tarte Flambée
- French Beef Stew (Daube de Boeuf)
- Leek and Potato Soup
- Tarte au Citron
- Crêpes Suzette
- Soupe à l'Oignon Gratinée
- Moussaka (French Style)
- Chateaubriand with Béarnaise Sauce
- Grilled Lamb Chops with Herb Butter

Croque Monsieur

Ingredients:

- 8 slices of white bread
- 4 slices of ham
- 4 slices of Gruyère cheese
- 2 tbsp Dijon mustard
- 2 tbsp butter (melted)
- ½ cup béchamel sauce (see below for the recipe)

Instructions:

1. Preheat your oven to 375°F (190°C).
2. Spread Dijon mustard on 4 slices of bread.
3. Layer a slice of ham and a slice of Gruyère cheese on top of the mustard.
4. Place the other 4 slices of bread on top to form sandwiches.
5. Brush the top of each sandwich with melted butter.
6. Spread béchamel sauce on top of each sandwich.
7. Bake for 10-15 minutes or until golden brown and crispy on the outside, and the cheese is melted inside.

Quiche Lorraine

Ingredients:

- 1 pre-made pie crust
- 6 large eggs
- 1 cup heavy cream
- 1 cup milk
- 1 ½ cups cooked bacon (chopped)
- 1 cup Gruyère cheese (shredded)
- 1 small onion (finely chopped)
- Salt and pepper to taste

Instructions:

1. Preheat the oven to 375°F (190°C).
2. In a skillet, sauté onions until soft, about 5 minutes.
3. In a mixing bowl, whisk eggs, cream, and milk together. Add salt and pepper.
4. Place bacon, sautéed onions, and cheese in the pie crust.
5. Pour the egg mixture over the ingredients in the crust.
6. Bake for 35-40 minutes or until set and lightly golden.
7. Let cool for a few minutes before slicing.

French Onion Soup

Ingredients:

- 4 large yellow onions (thinly sliced)
- 4 cups beef broth
- 1 cup white wine
- 2 tbsp butter
- 2 tbsp olive oil
- 2 tsp thyme leaves
- 2 bay leaves
- Salt and pepper to taste
- 8 slices of French baguette
- 2 cups Gruyère cheese (shredded)

Instructions:

1. In a large pot, melt butter and olive oil over medium heat.
2. Add onions and cook, stirring occasionally, for about 30-40 minutes until golden brown.
3. Add thyme, bay leaves, wine, and beef broth. Bring to a boil, then reduce heat and simmer for 30 minutes.
4. Season with salt and pepper to taste.
5. Meanwhile, toast the baguette slices.

6. Ladle soup into bowls, top with toasted baguette, and sprinkle with Gruyère cheese.

7. Broil in the oven for 2-3 minutes until cheese is bubbly and golden.

Ratatouille

Ingredients:

- 2 eggplants (diced)
- 2 zucchinis (sliced)
- 1 red bell pepper (diced)
- 1 yellow bell pepper (diced)
- 1 onion (diced)
- 2 tomatoes (diced)
- 2 tbsp olive oil
- 2 cloves garlic (minced)
- 1 tsp thyme
- 1 tsp basil
- Salt and pepper to taste

Instructions:

1. Heat olive oil in a large skillet over medium heat.
2. Add onions and garlic and cook until soft.
3. Add eggplant, zucchini, and bell peppers, and cook for 10 minutes, stirring occasionally.
4. Add tomatoes, thyme, basil, salt, and pepper.
5. Simmer for 20 minutes, stirring occasionally, until vegetables are tender.

6. Adjust seasoning, and serve hot.

Steak Frites

Ingredients:

- 2 ribeye or sirloin steaks
- 4 cups frozen French fries (or homemade)
- 2 tbsp olive oil
- 2 tbsp butter
- 2 cloves garlic (minced)
- 1 tbsp fresh parsley (chopped)
- Salt and pepper to taste

Instructions:

1. Cook the fries according to package instructions or fry them until golden and crispy.
2. Meanwhile, heat olive oil in a skillet over medium-high heat.
3. Season the steaks with salt and pepper, and cook for 3-4 minutes per side for medium-rare, or to your desired doneness.
4. Remove the steaks from the skillet and let rest.
5. In the same skillet, melt butter and sauté garlic for 1 minute.
6. Drizzle the garlic butter over the steaks and sprinkle with chopped parsley.
7. Serve with the fries on the side.

Coq au Vin

Ingredients:

- 1 whole chicken (cut into pieces)
- 1 bottle red wine
- 2 tbsp olive oil
- 1 onion (chopped)
- 2 carrots (sliced)
- 2 cloves garlic (minced)
- 1 cup chicken broth
- 1 tsp thyme
- 2 tbsp butter
- 8 oz mushrooms (sliced)
- Salt and pepper to taste

Instructions:

1. In a large pot, heat olive oil over medium heat. Brown the chicken pieces on all sides, then remove and set aside.
2. In the same pot, sauté onions, carrots, and garlic for 5 minutes.
3. Add wine, chicken broth, thyme, and salt and pepper. Bring to a simmer.
4. Return the chicken to the pot and cover. Cook for 45 minutes, stirring occasionally.
5. In a separate pan, melt butter and sauté mushrooms until golden.

6. Add the mushrooms to the pot, and cook for an additional 10 minutes.

7. Serve with crusty bread.

Duck Confit

Ingredients:

- 4 duck legs
- 4 cups duck fat (or enough to submerge the duck)
- 2 cloves garlic (crushed)
- 2 sprigs thyme
- 2 bay leaves
- Salt and pepper to taste

Instructions:

1. Season duck legs with salt and pepper.
2. In a large pot, melt duck fat over low heat.
3. Add garlic, thyme, and bay leaves, and submerge the duck legs in the fat.
4. Simmer on low heat for 2-3 hours until the duck is tender.
5. Remove the duck from the fat and crisp the skin in a hot skillet for 2-3 minutes.
6. Serve with vegetables or potatoes.

Beef Bourguignon

Ingredients:

- 2 lbs beef chuck (cut into cubes)
- 1 bottle red wine (preferably Burgundy)
- 2 tbsp olive oil
- 1 onion (chopped)
- 2 carrots (sliced)
- 2 cloves garlic (minced)
- 1 tsp thyme
- 2 bay leaves
- 2 cups beef broth
- 2 tbsp butter
- 8 oz mushrooms (sliced)
- Salt and pepper to taste

Instructions:

1. Heat olive oil in a large pot over medium-high heat. Brown the beef in batches and remove.
2. In the same pot, sauté onions, carrots, and garlic for 5 minutes.
3. Add wine, beef broth, thyme, bay leaves, and the beef back to the pot.
4. Bring to a simmer, then cover and cook for 2-3 hours until the beef is tender.

5. In a separate pan, melt butter and sauté mushrooms until golden.

6. Add mushrooms to the beef and cook for an additional 10 minutes.

7. Serve with mashed potatoes or crusty bread.

Escargots de Bourgogne

Ingredients:

- 24 escargots (canned or fresh)
- 4 tbsp unsalted butter (softened)
- 2 cloves garlic (minced)
- 2 tbsp parsley (chopped)
- 1 tbsp shallots (finely chopped)
- 1 tbsp white wine
- Salt and pepper to taste
- 1 baguette (sliced) for serving

Instructions:

1. Preheat your oven to 375°F (190°C).
2. In a small bowl, mix the softened butter, garlic, parsley, shallots, white wine, salt, and pepper.
3. Place the escargots in their shells or a baking dish.
4. Spoon the garlic butter mixture onto each escargot.
5. Bake for 10-12 minutes until the butter is bubbling and the escargots are hot.
6. Serve with slices of baguette to soak up the delicious garlic butter.

Moules Marinières

Ingredients:

- 2 lbs mussels (scrubbed and debearded)
- 2 tbsp butter
- 1 small onion (finely chopped)
- 2 cloves garlic (minced)
- 1 cup dry white wine
- 1 cup heavy cream
- 1 tbsp parsley (chopped)
- Salt and pepper to taste

Instructions:

1. In a large pot, melt butter over medium heat.
2. Add onion and garlic, cooking until softened, about 5 minutes.
3. Add the mussels, white wine, and a pinch of salt. Cover the pot and cook for about 5 minutes until the mussels open.
4. Add the cream and parsley, and simmer for 3 more minutes.
5. Season with salt and pepper.
6. Serve hot with crusty bread to dip in the sauce.

Croissant Sandwiches

Ingredients:

- 4 fresh croissants
- 8 oz deli meat (ham, turkey, or roast beef)
- 4 slices cheese (Swiss, cheddar, or your choice)
- Lettuce, tomato, and pickles (optional)
- Mustard or mayonnaise (optional)

Instructions:

1. Slice the croissants in half lengthwise.
2. Layer the deli meat, cheese, lettuce, tomato, and pickles inside each croissant.
3. Spread mustard or mayonnaise if desired.
4. Serve immediately or wrap them up for a picnic or lunch.

Gratin Dauphinois

Ingredients:

- 2 lbs potatoes (peeled and thinly sliced)
- 2 cups heavy cream
- 1 cup milk
- 2 cloves garlic (minced)
- 1 ½ cups Gruyère cheese (grated)
- 1 tsp thyme
- Salt and pepper to taste

Instructions:

1. Preheat your oven to 375°F (190°C).
2. In a saucepan, combine the heavy cream, milk, garlic, thyme, salt, and pepper. Bring to a simmer.
3. Layer the sliced potatoes in a buttered baking dish, pouring the cream mixture over each layer.
4. Top with grated Gruyère cheese.
5. Cover with foil and bake for 45 minutes. Remove the foil and bake for another 20-25 minutes until golden and bubbly.
6. Let it cool for a few minutes before serving.

Salade Niçoise

Ingredients:

- 2 cups mixed greens
- 2 boiled potatoes (sliced)
- 1 cup green beans (blanched)
- 4 oz tuna (canned in olive oil)
- 2 hard-boiled eggs (sliced)
- 8 cherry tomatoes (halved)
- 1/4 cup Kalamata olives
- 1 tbsp capers
- 1 small red onion (sliced)
- 2 tbsp olive oil
- 1 tbsp red wine vinegar
- Salt and pepper to taste

Instructions:

1. Arrange the mixed greens, potatoes, green beans, tuna, eggs, tomatoes, olives, and capers on a large platter.
2. Drizzle with olive oil and red wine vinegar.
3. Season with salt and pepper to taste.
4. Serve chilled or at room temperature.

Poulet Rôti (Roast Chicken)

Ingredients:

- 1 whole chicken (about 4 lbs)
- 2 tbsp olive oil
- 2 tbsp butter (softened)
- 4 cloves garlic (minced)
- 1 lemon (cut into wedges)
- 1 bunch fresh thyme
- Salt and pepper to taste

Instructions:

1. Preheat your oven to 425°F (220°C).
2. Rub the chicken with olive oil, butter, minced garlic, salt, and pepper.
3. Stuff the chicken with lemon wedges and thyme.
4. Place the chicken on a roasting rack in a baking dish.
5. Roast for about 1 hour and 15 minutes, or until the internal temperature reaches 165°F (75°C).
6. Let rest for 10 minutes before carving.

Tarte Tatin

Ingredients:

- 6-8 apples (peeled, cored, and halved)
- 1/2 cup butter
- 1 cup sugar
- 1 sheet puff pastry (store-bought)
- 1 tsp cinnamon (optional)

Instructions:

1. Preheat your oven to 375°F (190°C).
2. In a skillet, melt the butter and sugar over medium heat, stirring occasionally, until it forms a caramel.
3. Arrange the apple halves in the skillet, cut-side down, and cook for 10 minutes until tender.
4. Sprinkle cinnamon (if using) over the apples.
5. Place the puff pastry over the apples, tucking the edges in around the apples.
6. Bake for 25-30 minutes until golden and puffed.
7. Let cool for 10 minutes before flipping the tart onto a plate. Serve warm.

Chateaubriand

Ingredients:

- 1 ½ lbs center-cut beef tenderloin
- 2 tbsp olive oil
- 2 tbsp butter
- 2 cloves garlic (minced)
- 1 tbsp fresh rosemary (chopped)
- Salt and pepper to taste
- ½ cup red wine (optional for sauce)

Instructions:

1. Preheat your oven to 400°F (200°C).
2. Heat olive oil in a skillet over high heat.
3. Sear the beef tenderloin on all sides until browned, about 2-3 minutes per side.
4. Transfer the beef to the oven and roast for 20-25 minutes for medium-rare.
5. While the beef is roasting, melt butter in the skillet, add garlic and rosemary, and sauté for 1 minute.
6. Remove the beef from the oven and let it rest for 10 minutes.
7. Slice the beef and serve with the garlic-rosemary butter sauce or a red wine reduction.

French Toast

Ingredients:

- 4 slices of thick bread (such as brioche or challah)
- 2 large eggs
- 1 cup milk
- 1 tsp vanilla extract
- 1 tbsp sugar
- 1/4 tsp salt
- Butter for frying
- Maple syrup or powdered sugar for serving

Instructions:

1. In a bowl, whisk together eggs, milk, vanilla extract, sugar, and salt.
2. Heat a skillet over medium heat and add a little butter to coat.
3. Dip the bread slices into the egg mixture, making sure both sides are soaked.
4. Fry the bread in the skillet for 2-3 minutes per side, until golden brown.
5. Serve hot with maple syrup or powdered sugar on top.

Bœuf en Croûte (Beef Wellington)

Ingredients:

- 2 lbs beef tenderloin (center-cut)
- 2 tbsp olive oil
- 1 tbsp Dijon mustard
- 8 oz mushrooms (finely chopped)
- 2 tbsp butter
- 1 tbsp fresh thyme (chopped)
- 12 slices prosciutto
- 1 sheet puff pastry
- 1 egg (beaten)
- Salt and pepper to taste

Instructions:

1. Preheat your oven to 400°F (200°C).
2. Sear the beef tenderloin in olive oil over high heat for 2-3 minutes per side. Let it cool, then brush with Dijon mustard.
3. Sauté the mushrooms in butter with thyme until soft and all moisture has evaporated. Let cool.
4. Lay the prosciutto on plastic wrap and spread the mushroom mixture over it. Place the beef on top and roll it up tightly.
5. Roll out the puff pastry and wrap the beef tightly, sealing the edges.

6. Brush the pastry with the beaten egg and place on a baking sheet.

7. Bake for 35-40 minutes, or until the pastry is golden brown. Let rest before slicing.

French-style Omelette

Ingredients:

- 3 eggs
- 1 tbsp butter
- Fresh herbs (chives, parsley, tarragon, or dill)
- Salt and pepper to taste

Instructions:

1. Whisk the eggs with salt, pepper, and fresh herbs.
2. Heat a non-stick skillet over medium-low heat and melt butter.
3. Pour the eggs into the skillet and let them cook without stirring.
4. As the edges set, gently lift with a spatula and tilt the pan to let the uncooked egg flow to the edges.
5. Once the omelette is mostly set, fold it in half and serve immediately.

Soupe au Pistou
Ingredients:

- 2 tbsp olive oil
- 1 onion (diced)
- 2 carrots (sliced)
- 2 zucchini (diced)
- 4 cups vegetable or chicken broth
- 1 can (15 oz) cannellini beans (drained and rinsed)
- 1/2 cup pasta (small shapes like ditalini)
- 2 cups fresh basil leaves
- 1/4 cup garlic (minced)
- 1/4 cup olive oil (for pistou)
- Salt and pepper to taste

Instructions:

1. Heat olive oil in a large pot over medium heat. Add onion, carrots, and zucchini. Cook until softened, about 5 minutes.
2. Add the broth, beans, and pasta, and bring to a boil. Simmer for 10 minutes until the pasta is tender.
3. In a blender or food processor, blend basil, garlic, and olive oil to make the pistou.
4. Stir the pistou into the soup, season with salt and pepper, and serve hot.

Pâté en Croûte

Ingredients:

- 1 lb ground pork
- 1/2 lb ground veal
- 1/2 lb ground beef
- 1/4 lb pork fat (or bacon)
- 1/2 cup dry white wine
- 1/4 cup brandy
- 1/4 tsp nutmeg
- 1/4 tsp cinnamon
- Salt and pepper to taste
- 1 sheet puff pastry

Instructions:

1. Preheat your oven to 350°F (175°C).
2. In a bowl, mix all meats, fat, wine, brandy, spices, salt, and pepper.
3. Line a loaf pan with puff pastry, leaving extra around the edges.
4. Fill the pastry with the meat mixture, pressing it down to compact.
5. Fold the pastry over to cover the top, sealing the edges.
6. Bake for 1-1.5 hours until golden and cooked through. Let rest before slicing.

Galette Bretonne

Ingredients:

- 1 cup buckwheat flour
- 1/4 cup all-purpose flour
- 1/2 tsp salt
- 1 large egg
- 1 cup water
- 1 tbsp butter (melted)
- Filling of choice (cheese, ham, egg, mushrooms, spinach, etc.)

Instructions:

1. In a bowl, whisk together buckwheat flour, all-purpose flour, salt, egg, and water until smooth.
2. Heat a skillet over medium heat and lightly grease with butter.
3. Pour in a small amount of batter and tilt the pan to spread it thinly.
4. Cook for 2-3 minutes, then flip and cook for another 2-3 minutes.
5. Add the filling of your choice and fold the edges of the galette over the filling. Serve immediately.

Croque Madame

Ingredients:

- 2 slices of bread (preferably brioche or country bread)
- 4 slices of ham
- 2 slices of Swiss or Gruyère cheese
- 1 egg
- 1 tbsp butter
- 1 tbsp Dijon mustard
- 1/2 cup béchamel sauce (optional)

Instructions:

1. Toast the bread slices and spread mustard on one side of each.
2. Place a slice of cheese, a slice of ham, and another slice of cheese on one piece of toast.
3. Top with the second slice of toast.
4. In a skillet, melt butter and cook the sandwich on both sides until golden brown and the cheese has melted.
5. Fry the egg in the skillet and place it on top of the sandwich. Serve immediately.

Cassoulet

Ingredients:

- 1 lb white beans (such as cannellini)
- 4 sausages (preferably Toulouse sausage)
- 1 lb pork shoulder (cubed)
- 4 slices bacon (diced)
- 1 onion (diced)
- 2 cloves garlic (minced)
- 4 cups chicken broth
- 2 cups tomatoes (diced)
- 1 bay leaf
- 1 tsp thyme
- Salt and pepper to taste

Instructions:

1. Soak the beans overnight and drain them.
2. In a large pot, cook the bacon and sausages until browned. Remove and set aside.
3. In the same pot, cook the pork shoulder until browned.
4. Add onion, garlic, and tomatoes, cooking until softened.
5. Add the beans, chicken broth, bay leaf, and thyme. Bring to a boil, then reduce to a simmer.

6. Let cook for 2-3 hours, adding more broth if necessary, until the beans are tender and the flavors have melded.

Pissaladière

Ingredients:

- 1 pizza dough or puff pastry sheet
- 2 large onions (thinly sliced)
- 2 tbsp olive oil
- 1/4 cup black olives (pitted)
- 4 anchovies (optional)
- 1 tbsp fresh thyme

Instructions:

1. Preheat your oven to 400°F (200°C).
2. Heat olive oil in a skillet over medium heat. Add the onions and cook for 15-20 minutes until soft and caramelized.
3. Roll out the pizza dough or puff pastry on a baking sheet.
4. Spread the caramelized onions on top, then top with olives, anchovies, and thyme.
5. Bake for 15-20 minutes, until the crust is golden brown. Serve warm.

Foie Gras

Ingredients:

- 1 lb foie gras (liver)
- Salt and pepper to taste
- 1/2 cup brandy or cognac
- 1/4 cup vegetable oil
- Fresh herbs (thyme, rosemary)

Instructions:

1. Preheat the oven to 350°F (175°C).
2. Season the foie gras with salt and pepper.
3. Heat a skillet over medium-high heat and sear the foie gras on both sides for 2-3 minutes until golden.
4. Place the foie gras in an oven-safe dish, drizzle with brandy, and add fresh herbs.
5. Roast in the oven for 5-10 minutes, then let it rest before serving.

Salmon en Papillote

Ingredients:

- 2 salmon fillets
- 1 lemon (sliced)
- Fresh herbs (dill or parsley)
- 1 tbsp olive oil
- Salt and pepper to taste
- Parchment paper

Instructions:

1. Preheat your oven to 375°F (190°C).
2. Cut parchment paper into large squares. Place a salmon fillet in the center of each square.
3. Drizzle with olive oil, then add lemon slices, fresh herbs, and seasoning.
4. Fold the parchment over the fish to create a sealed packet.
5. Bake for 15-20 minutes until the salmon is cooked through. Serve hot.

Clafoutis

Ingredients:

- 2 cups cherries (pitted)
- 3 large eggs
- 1 cup milk
- 1/2 cup sugar
- 1/2 cup flour
- 1 tsp vanilla extract
- Pinch of salt
- Powdered sugar for garnish

Instructions:

1. Preheat the oven to 350°F (175°C).
2. Butter a baking dish and arrange the cherries in the bottom.
3. In a bowl, whisk together eggs, milk, sugar, flour, vanilla, and salt until smooth.
4. Pour the batter over the cherries.
5. Bake for 35-40 minutes until golden and set.
6. Dust with powdered sugar and serve warm or at room temperature.

Endives au Gratin

Ingredients:

- 4 endives
- 1 tbsp butter
- 1 tbsp flour
- 1 cup milk
- 1/2 cup grated Gruyère or Swiss cheese
- Salt and pepper to taste
- 1/4 cup breadcrumbs

Instructions:

1. Preheat the oven to 375°F (190°C).
2. Trim the endives and cook them in boiling salted water for 10 minutes. Drain and set aside.
3. In a saucepan, melt butter over medium heat and stir in flour. Gradually add milk, whisking until the sauce thickens.
4. Stir in cheese, salt, and pepper.
5. Place the endives in a baking dish and pour the sauce over them. Sprinkle with breadcrumbs.
6. Bake for 20 minutes, until golden and bubbly.

Blanquette de Veau

Ingredients:

- 2 lbs veal (cut into cubes)
- 1 onion (halved)
- 2 carrots (sliced)
- 3 cups chicken broth
- 1 cup white wine
- 1/4 cup flour
- 2 tbsp butter
- 1/2 cup heavy cream
- 1 tbsp lemon juice
- Fresh parsley (chopped)

Instructions:

1. Brown the veal cubes in a large pot. Add onions and carrots and cook for 5 minutes.

2. Add the chicken broth and white wine. Bring to a boil, then reduce to a simmer. Cook for 1-1.5 hours until the meat is tender.

3. In a separate pan, melt butter and stir in flour to make a roux. Slowly add the cooking liquid from the veal, whisking until thickened.

4. Stir in heavy cream, lemon juice, and fresh parsley.

5. Pour the sauce over the veal and serve hot.

Pâtisserie au Chocolat

Ingredients:

- 1 sheet puff pastry
- 1/2 cup chocolate (chopped)
- 1 egg (beaten)
- 2 tbsp sugar

Instructions:

1. Preheat the oven to 400°F (200°C).
2. Roll out the puff pastry and cut into small squares.
3. Place a piece of chocolate in the center of each square and fold the edges over to seal.
4. Brush the pastry with beaten egg and sprinkle with sugar.
5. Bake for 12-15 minutes until golden and puffed.

Pommes Frites

Ingredients:

- 4 large potatoes (peeled and cut into thin fries)
- 4 cups vegetable oil
- Salt to taste

Instructions:

1. Preheat oil in a deep fryer or large pot to 350°F (175°C).
2. Fry the potatoes in batches for 3-5 minutes until golden brown and crispy.
3. Drain on paper towels and season with salt immediately. Serve hot.

Soufflé au Fromage

Ingredients:

- 1/4 cup butter
- 1/4 cup flour
- 1 cup milk
- 1 1/2 cups grated Gruyère cheese
- 4 large eggs (separated)
- Salt and pepper to taste

Instructions:

1. Preheat your oven to 375°F (190°C).
2. In a saucepan, melt butter and stir in flour. Gradually add milk and cook until thickened.
3. Stir in cheese and season with salt and pepper. Remove from heat and let cool slightly.
4. Beat the egg whites to stiff peaks and fold them into the cheese mixture.
5. Pour into a buttered soufflé dish and bake for 25-30 minutes until puffed and golden.

Chouquettes

Ingredients:

- 1/2 cup water
- 1/2 cup unsalted butter
- 1 cup all-purpose flour
- 4 large eggs
- 1 tbsp sugar
- Pinch of salt
- Pearl sugar (for topping)

Instructions:

1. Preheat your oven to 375°F (190°C).
2. In a saucepan, bring water, butter, and a pinch of salt to a boil.
3. Stir in the flour and cook for 1-2 minutes until the mixture forms a dough.
4. Remove from heat and let it cool for a few minutes. Gradually add the eggs, one at a time, mixing well after each addition.
5. Drop spoonfuls of dough onto a baking sheet lined with parchment paper. Sprinkle with pearl sugar.
6. Bake for 20-25 minutes until golden and puffed. Let cool and serve.

Grilled Ratatouille Sandwich
Ingredients:

- 1 cup zucchini (sliced)
- 1 cup eggplant (sliced)
- 1 cup bell pepper (sliced)
- 1/2 cup onion (sliced)
- 2 tbsp olive oil
- 2 cloves garlic (minced)
- 2 slices French baguette
- 1 tbsp pesto
- Salt and pepper to taste

Instructions:

1. Preheat the grill or grill pan.
2. Toss the sliced vegetables in olive oil, salt, pepper, and garlic. Grill the vegetables for 4-5 minutes on each side until tender and charred.
3. Toast the baguette slices on the grill.
4. Spread pesto on one side of each toasted baguette.
5. Layer the grilled vegetables on one slice and top with the other slice. Serve warm.

Pain Perdu (French Toast)

Ingredients:

- 4 slices day-old bread (brioche or challah works best)
- 2 large eggs
- 1/2 cup milk
- 1 tbsp sugar
- 1 tsp vanilla extract
- 1/4 tsp cinnamon
- Butter (for cooking)
- Powdered sugar and maple syrup for serving

Instructions:

1. In a bowl, whisk together eggs, milk, sugar, vanilla, and cinnamon.
2. Heat a pan with butter over medium heat.
3. Dip the bread slices into the egg mixture, ensuring both sides are coated.
4. Cook each slice in the pan for 2-3 minutes per side, until golden brown.
5. Serve with powdered sugar and maple syrup.

Salade de Chèvre Chaud

Ingredients:

- 4 slices goat cheese
- 1 tbsp honey
- 2 tbsp olive oil
- 1 tsp thyme
- 4 cups mixed greens
- 1/4 red onion (sliced)
- 1/2 cup walnuts (toasted)
- Balsamic vinegar

Instructions:

1. Preheat the oven to 375°F (190°C).
2. Place the goat cheese slices on a baking sheet lined with parchment paper. Drizzle with honey and olive oil, then sprinkle with thyme.
3. Bake for 5-7 minutes until the cheese is warm and slightly golden.
4. Toss the mixed greens, red onion, and walnuts in a bowl.
5. Plate the salad and top with the warm goat cheese. Drizzle with balsamic vinegar and serve.

Mousse au Chocolat

Ingredients:

- 8 oz dark chocolate (chopped)
- 2 tbsp butter
- 4 large eggs (separated)
- 1/4 cup sugar
- 1 cup heavy cream

Instructions:

1. Melt the chocolate and butter together in a heatproof bowl over simmering water, stirring until smooth.
2. Whisk the egg yolks with sugar until pale and thick.
3. In a separate bowl, whip the heavy cream to stiff peaks.
4. Fold the chocolate into the egg yolk mixture, then gently fold in the whipped cream.
5. Beat the egg whites to stiff peaks and fold them into the mousse.
6. Spoon into serving glasses and refrigerate for 2 hours before serving.

Bouillabaisse

Ingredients:

- 1 lb mixed fish fillets (such as cod, halibut, or bass)
- 1/2 lb shrimp (peeled and deveined)
- 1 onion (chopped)
- 2 leeks (sliced)
- 2 tomatoes (chopped)
- 1 tbsp olive oil
- 4 cups fish stock
- 1/2 cup white wine
- 1/4 tsp saffron threads
- 2 cloves garlic (minced)
- 1 bay leaf
- Salt and pepper to taste
- Fresh parsley (chopped)

Instructions:

1. In a large pot, heat olive oil and sauté onion, leeks, and garlic until softened.
2. Add tomatoes, fish stock, white wine, saffron, and bay leaf. Bring to a boil, then reduce the heat and simmer for 20 minutes.
3. Add the fish and shrimp to the pot, season with salt and pepper, and simmer for another 10 minutes until the seafood is cooked through.

4. Remove the bay leaf, then serve the bouillabaisse with fresh parsley and crusty bread.

French Garlic Butter Shrimp

Ingredients:

- 1 lb shrimp (peeled and deveined)
- 4 tbsp unsalted butter
- 5 cloves garlic (minced)
- 1 tbsp fresh parsley (chopped)
- Juice of 1 lemon
- Salt and pepper to taste

Instructions:

1. In a skillet, melt butter over medium heat. Add garlic and cook for 1-2 minutes until fragrant.
2. Add shrimp and cook for 3-4 minutes on each side until pink and cooked through.
3. Stir in lemon juice and fresh parsley. Season with salt and pepper.
4. Serve with crusty bread for dipping.

Potatoes Lyonnaise

Ingredients:

- 2 lbs potatoes (peeled and sliced thin)
- 1/2 cup butter
- 1/2 cup onion (thinly sliced)
- 2 tbsp fresh parsley (chopped)
- Salt and pepper to taste

Instructions:

1. Boil the sliced potatoes in salted water until tender, about 10 minutes. Drain and set aside.
2. In a large skillet, melt butter over medium heat and sauté onions until golden and soft.
3. Add the potatoes to the skillet and cook for 5-7 minutes until crispy and browned.
4. Season with salt, pepper, and fresh parsley. Serve hot.

Tarte Flambée

Ingredients:

- 1 pizza dough or puff pastry (store-bought or homemade)
- 1/2 cup crème fraîche
- 1 small onion (thinly sliced)
- 4 oz lardons (bacon strips)
- 1/2 cup grated Gruyère cheese
- Salt and pepper to taste

Instructions:

1. Preheat your oven to 475°F (245°C).
2. Roll out the pizza dough or puff pastry to fit a baking sheet.
3. Spread a thin layer of crème fraîche over the dough, leaving a small border around the edges.
4. Scatter the sliced onions, lardons, and Gruyère cheese on top.
5. Season with salt and pepper.
6. Bake for 10-12 minutes, or until the edges are golden and crispy.
7. Slice and serve warm.

French Beef Stew (Daube de Boeuf)

Ingredients:

- 2 lbs beef stew meat (chuck or brisket)
- 2 onions (chopped)
- 2 carrots (sliced)
- 4 cloves garlic (minced)
- 2 tbsp tomato paste
- 1 cup red wine
- 3 cups beef broth
- 2 tbsp olive oil
- 1 bouquet garni (parsley, thyme, bay leaves)
- Salt and pepper to taste

Instructions:

1. Heat olive oil in a large pot over medium-high heat. Brown the beef in batches and set aside.
2. In the same pot, sauté the onions, carrots, and garlic until softened.
3. Stir in the tomato paste and cook for 1-2 minutes.
4. Add the beef back to the pot, then pour in the wine and beef broth.
5. Add the bouquet garni and season with salt and pepper.
6. Bring to a boil, then reduce the heat and simmer for 2-3 hours until the beef is tender.

7. Discard the bouquet garni and serve hot with crusty bread.

Leek and Potato Soup

Ingredients:

- 3 leeks (cleaned and sliced)
- 4 potatoes (peeled and diced)
- 4 cups chicken or vegetable broth
- 1/2 cup heavy cream
- 2 tbsp butter
- Salt and pepper to taste

Instructions:

1. Melt the butter in a large pot over medium heat. Add the leeks and cook until soft.
2. Add the potatoes and cook for 5 minutes, stirring occasionally.
3. Pour in the broth, bring to a boil, then reduce the heat and simmer for 20 minutes, until the potatoes are tender.
4. Use an immersion blender to blend the soup until smooth.
5. Stir in the cream and season with salt and pepper.
6. Serve hot with a sprinkle of chives.

Tarte au Citron

Ingredients:

- 1 pre-baked tart shell
- 1 cup granulated sugar
- 3 large eggs
- 2/3 cup fresh lemon juice
- 1/2 cup heavy cream
- Zest of 2 lemons
- 1/4 cup butter (cubed)

Instructions:

1. Preheat the oven to 350°F (175°C).
2. Whisk together the sugar, eggs, and lemon juice in a bowl.
3. In a saucepan, combine the lemon zest and cream. Heat over low heat until warm.
4. Slowly pour the warm cream mixture into the egg mixture, whisking constantly.
5. Pour the mixture back into the saucepan and cook over medium heat until thickened.
6. Remove from heat and stir in the butter.
7. Pour the filling into the pre-baked tart shell and bake for 10-12 minutes.
8. Let cool before serving.

Crêpes Suzette

Ingredients:

- 1 batch of crêpe batter (see below)
- 1/4 cup unsalted butter
- 1/4 cup orange juice
- Zest of 1 orange
- 1/4 cup orange liqueur (such as Grand Marnier)
- 2 tbsp sugar

Crêpe Batter:

- 1 cup all-purpose flour
- 1 tbsp sugar
- 2 large eggs
- 1 1/2 cups milk
- 2 tbsp melted butter
- Pinch of salt

Instructions:

1. For the crêpes, whisk all ingredients together until smooth. Heat a non-stick pan and lightly butter it. Pour in a small amount of batter, swirling it around to form a thin layer. Cook for 1-2 minutes, then flip and cook the other side. Set aside.

2. In a large skillet, melt the butter over medium heat. Add orange juice, zest, and sugar, and cook until the sauce thickens slightly.

3. Fold the crêpes into quarters and add them to the skillet.

4. Pour in the orange liqueur and flame it (carefully light the alcohol with a match, then let it burn off).

5. Serve the crêpes warm with extra sauce.

Soupe à l'Oignon Gratinée

Ingredients:

- 4 large onions (thinly sliced)
- 4 cups beef broth
- 2 tbsp butter
- 2 tbsp olive oil
- 1/2 cup white wine
- 2 tbsp flour
- 4 slices French bread
- 1 1/2 cups grated Gruyère cheese
- Salt and pepper to taste

Instructions:

1. In a large pot, melt the butter and olive oil over medium heat. Add the onions and cook, stirring occasionally, for about 30 minutes, until the onions are caramelized.
2. Stir in the flour and cook for 1-2 minutes.
3. Add the wine, scraping up any bits from the bottom of the pot.
4. Pour in the broth, bring to a simmer, and cook for 20 minutes. Season with salt and pepper.
5. Preheat the oven to 400°F (200°C).
6. Place the French bread slices on a baking sheet and toast in the oven for 5 minutes.

7. Ladle the soup into oven-safe bowls, top with a slice of toast, and sprinkle with cheese.

8. Place the bowls under the broiler for 2-3 minutes until the cheese is melted and golden. Serve immediately.

Moussaka (French Style)

Ingredients:

- 2 eggplants (sliced)
- 1 lb ground lamb or beef
- 1 onion (chopped)
- 2 garlic cloves (minced)
- 1 can (14 oz) crushed tomatoes
- 1 tsp cinnamon
- 1/2 cup red wine
- 1/2 cup béchamel sauce (see below)
- 1/4 cup grated Parmesan cheese
- Olive oil for cooking

Béchamel Sauce:

- 2 tbsp butter
- 2 tbsp flour
- 1 cup milk
- Salt and pepper to taste

Instructions:

1. Preheat the oven to 375°F (190°C).

2. Slice the eggplants and grill or fry them until tender. Set aside.

3. In a pan, sauté the onion and garlic until softened. Add the ground meat and cook until browned.

4. Stir in the crushed tomatoes, red wine, cinnamon, salt, and pepper. Simmer for 20 minutes.

5. For the béchamel sauce, melt butter in a saucepan, stir in the flour, and cook for 1-2 minutes. Gradually add milk, whisking until thickened.

6. In a baking dish, layer the eggplant slices, then top with the meat sauce and a layer of béchamel.

7. Sprinkle with Parmesan cheese and bake for 30 minutes until golden and bubbly.

Chateaubriand with Béarnaise Sauce
Ingredients:

- 2 lb Chateaubriand (center-cut beef tenderloin)
- 2 tbsp olive oil
- Salt and pepper to taste

Béarnaise Sauce:

- 1/4 cup white wine vinegar
- 1/4 cup white wine
- 1/4 cup shallots (finely chopped)
- 3 egg yolks
- 1 cup unsalted butter (melted)
- 1 tbsp fresh tarragon (chopped)
- Salt and pepper to taste

Instructions:

1. Preheat your oven to 400°F (200°C).
2. Rub the beef with olive oil, salt, and pepper.
3. Sear the beef in a hot skillet for 2-3 minutes per side.
4. Transfer the skillet to the oven and roast for 20-25 minutes for medium-rare.
5. For the Béarnaise sauce, combine vinegar, wine, and shallots in a pan and reduce by half.

6. Whisk the egg yolks in a bowl, then slowly add the reduced vinegar mixture.

7. Gradually whisk in the melted butter, then stir in the tarragon and season with salt and pepper.

8. Serve the Chateaubriand with the Béarnaise sauce.

Grilled Lamb Chops with Herb Butter

Ingredients:

- 8 lamb chops
- 2 tbsp olive oil
- 1 tbsp garlic (minced)
- 1 tbsp fresh rosemary (chopped)

4o mini

ChatGPT said:

- 1/2 tsp salt
- 1/2 tsp pepper

Herb Butter:

- 1/4 cup unsalted butter (softened)
- 1 tbsp fresh parsley (chopped)
- 1 tbsp fresh thyme (chopped)
- 1 tsp lemon zest

Instructions:

1. Preheat your grill to medium-high heat.
2. Rub the lamb chops with olive oil, garlic, rosemary, salt, and pepper.
3. Grill the chops for 3-4 minutes per side for medium-rare.

4. For the herb butter, mix all ingredients together and refrigerate until firm.

5. Serve the lamb chops with a dollop of herb butter.

www.ingramcontent.com/pod-product-compliance
Lightning Source LLC
LaVergne TN
LVHW081318060526
838201LV00055B/2343